Love to stir THINGS UP

These Family Recipes Belong To:

Recipe

Page #

Recipe	Page #

Recipe

Page #

Recipe For:

_____

Ingredients:

_____

_____

_____

_____

_____

Directions:

_____

_____

_____

_____

_____

_____

_____

_____

_____

_____

_____

Notes:

_____

_____

_____

_____

_____

_____

_____

_____

_____

_____

_____

_____

_____

_____

_____

_____

From The Kitchen Of:

_____

Recipe For:

_____

Ingredients:

_____

_____

_____

_____

_____

Directions:

_____

_____

_____

_____

_____

_____

_____

_____

_____

_____

_____

Notes:

_____

_____

_____

_____

_____

_____

_____

_____

_____

_____

_____

_____

_____

_____

_____

_____

From The Kitchen Of:

_____

Recipe For:

_____

Ingredients:

_____

_____

_____

_____

_____

Directions:

_____

_____

_____

_____

_____

_____

_____

_____

_____

_____

_____

Notes:

_____

_____

_____

_____

_____

_____

_____

_____

_____

_____

_____

_____

_____

_____

From The Kitchen Of:

_____

Recipe For:

_____

Ingredients:

_____

_____

_____

_____

_____

Directions:

_____

_____

_____

_____

_____

_____

_____

_____

_____

_____

Notes:

_____

_____

_____

_____

_____

_____

_____

_____

_____

_____

_____

_____

_____

_____

_____

_____

From The Kitchen Of:

_____

Recipe For:

_____

Ingredients:

_____

_____

_____

_____

_____

Directions:

_____

_____

_____

_____

_____

_____

_____

_____

_____

_____

Notes:

_____

_____

_____

_____

_____

_____

_____

_____

_____

_____

_____

_____

_____

_____

_____

From The Kitchen Of:

_____

Recipe For:

_____

Ingredients:

_____

_____

_____

_____

_____

Directions:

_____

_____

_____

_____

_____

_____

_____

_____

_____

_____

Notes:

_____

_____

_____

_____

_____

_____

_____

_____

_____

_____

_____

_____

_____

_____

From The Kitchen Of:

_____

Recipe For:

_____

Ingredients:

_____

_____

_____

_____

_____

Directions:

_____

_____

_____

_____

_____

_____

_____

_____

_____

_____

Notes:

_____

_____

_____

_____

_____

_____

_____

_____

_____

_____

_____

_____

_____

_____

_____

_____

From The Kitchen Of:

_____

Recipe For:

_____

Ingredients:

_____

_____

_____

_____

_____

Directions:

_____

_____

_____

_____

_____

_____

_____

_____

_____

_____

_____

Notes:

_____

_____

_____

_____

_____

_____

_____

_____

_____

_____

_____

_____

_____

_____

_____

_____

From The Kitchen Of:

_____

Recipe For:

_____

Ingredients:

_____

_____

_____

_____

_____

Directions:

_____

_____

_____

_____

_____

_____

_____

_____

_____

_____

Notes:

_____

_____

_____

_____

_____

_____

_____

_____

_____

_____

_____

_____

_____

_____

From The Kitchen Of:

_____

Recipe For:

_____

Ingredients:

_____

_____

_____

_____

_____

Directions:

_____

_____

_____

_____

_____

_____

_____

_____

_____

_____

_____

Notes:

_____

_____

_____

_____

_____

_____

_____

_____

_____

_____

_____

_____

_____

_____

From The Kitchen Of:

_____

Recipe For:

_____

Ingredients:

_____

_____

_____

_____

_____

Directions:

_____

_____

_____

_____

_____

_____

_____

_____

_____

_____

Notes:

_____

_____

_____

_____

_____

_____

_____

_____

_____

_____

_____

_____

_____

_____

From The Kitchen Of:

_____

Recipe For:

_____

Ingredients:

_____

_____

_____

_____

_____

Directions:

_____

_____

_____

_____

_____

_____

_____

_____

_____

_____

Notes:

_____

_____

_____

_____

_____

_____

_____

_____

_____

_____

_____

_____

_____

_____

_____

From The Kitchen Of:

_____

Recipe For:

_____

Ingredients:

_____

_____

_____

_____

_____

Directions:

_____

_____

_____

_____

_____

_____

_____

_____

_____

_____

Notes:

_____

_____

_____

_____

_____

_____

_____

_____

_____

_____

_____

_____

_____

_____

_____

_____

From The Kitchen Of:

_____

Recipe For:

_____

Ingredients:

_____

_____

_____

_____

_____

Directions:

_____

_____

_____

_____

_____

_____

_____

_____

_____

_____

Notes:

_____

_____

_____

_____

_____

_____

_____

_____

_____

_____

_____

_____

_____

_____

_____

From The Kitchen Of:

_____

Recipe For:

_____

Ingredients:

_____

_____

_____

_____

_____

Directions:

_____

_____

_____

_____

_____

_____

_____

_____

_____

_____

Notes:

_____

_____

_____

_____

_____

_____

_____

_____

_____

_____

_____

_____

_____

_____

_____

From The Kitchen Of:

_____

Recipe For:

_____

Ingredients:

_____

_____

_____

_____

_____

Directions:

_____

_____

_____

_____

_____

_____

_____

_____

_____

_____

Notes:

_____

_____

_____

_____

_____

_____

_____

_____

_____

_____

_____

_____

_____

_____

_____

_____

From The Kitchen Of:

_____

Recipe For:

_____

Ingredients:

_____

_____

_____

_____

_____

Directions:

_____

_____

_____

_____

_____

_____

_____

_____

_____

_____

Notes:

_____

_____

_____

_____

_____

_____

_____

_____

_____

_____

_____

_____

_____

_____

_____

_____

From The Kitchen Of:

_____

Recipe For:

_____

Ingredients:

_____

_____

_____

_____

_____

Directions:

_____

_____

_____

_____

_____

_____

_____

_____

_____

_____

Notes:

_____

_____

_____

_____

_____

_____

_____

_____

_____

_____

_____

_____

_____

_____

_____

From The Kitchen Of:

_____

Recipe For:

_____

Ingredients:

_____

_____

_____

_____

_____

Directions:

_____

_____

_____

_____

_____

_____

_____

_____

_____

_____

Notes:

_____

_____

_____

_____

_____

_____

_____

_____

_____

_____

_____

_____

_____

_____

_____

From The Kitchen Of:

_____

Recipe For:

_____

Ingredients:

_____

_____

_____

_____

_____

Directions:

_____

_____

_____

_____

_____

_____

_____

_____

_____

_____

_____

Notes:

_____

_____

_____

_____

_____

_____

_____

_____

_____

_____

_____

_____

_____

_____

_____

_____

From The Kitchen Of:

_____

Recipe For:

_____

Ingredients:

_____

_____

_____

_____

_____

Directions:

_____

_____

_____

_____

_____

_____

_____

_____

_____

_____

Notes:

_____

_____

_____

_____

_____

_____

_____

_____

_____

_____

_____

_____

_____

_____

_____

_____

From The Kitchen Of:

_____

Recipe For:

_____

Ingredients:

_____

_____

_____

_____

_____

Directions:

_____

_____

_____

_____

_____

_____

_____

_____

_____

_____

Notes:

_____

_____

_____

_____

_____

_____

_____

_____

_____

_____

_____

_____

_____

_____

From The Kitchen Of:

_____

Recipe For:

_____

Ingredients:

_____

_____

_____

_____

_____

Directions:

_____

_____

_____

_____

_____

_____

_____

_____

_____

_____

Notes:

_____

_____

_____

_____

_____

_____

_____

_____

_____

_____

_____

_____

_____

_____

_____

_____

From The Kitchen Of:

_____

Recipe For:

_____

Ingredients:

_____

_____

_____

_____

_____

Directions:

_____

_____

_____

_____

_____

_____

_____

_____

_____

_____

Notes:

_____

_____

_____

_____

_____

_____

_____

_____

_____

_____

_____

_____

_____

_____

_____

_____

From The Kitchen Of:

_____

Recipe For:

_____

Ingredients:

_____

_____

_____

_____

_____

Directions:

_____

_____

_____

_____

_____

_____

_____

_____

_____

_____

_____

Notes:

_____

_____

_____

_____

_____

_____

_____

_____

_____

_____

_____

_____

_____

_____

_____

From The Kitchen Of:

_____

Recipe For:

_____

Ingredients:

_____
_____
_____
_____
_____

Directions:

_____
_____
_____
_____
_____
_____
_____
_____
_____
_____
_____

Notes:

_____

_____

_____

_____

_____

_____

_____

_____

_____

_____

_____

_____

_____

_____

_____

_____

_____

From The Kitchen Of:

_____

Recipe For:

_____

Ingredients:

_____

_____

_____

_____

_____

Directions:

_____

_____

_____

_____

_____

_____

_____

_____

_____

_____

Notes:

_____

_____

_____

_____

_____

_____

_____

_____

_____

_____

_____

_____

_____

_____

_____

_____

From The Kitchen Of:

_____

Recipe For:

_____

Ingredients:

_____
_____
_____
_____
_____

Directions:

_____
_____
_____
_____
_____
_____
_____
_____
_____
_____

Notes:

_____

_____

_____

_____

_____

_____

_____

_____

_____

_____

_____

_____

_____

_____

_____

From The Kitchen Of:

_____

Recipe For:

_____

Ingredients:

_____

_____

_____

_____

_____

Directions:

_____

_____

_____

_____

_____

_____

_____

_____

_____

_____

_____

Notes:

_____

_____

_____

_____

_____

_____

_____

_____

_____

_____

_____

_____

_____

_____

_____

_____

From The Kitchen Of:

_____

Recipe For:

_____

Ingredients:

_____

_____

_____

_____

_____

Directions:

_____

_____

_____

_____

_____

_____

_____

_____

_____

_____

Notes:

_____

_____

_____

_____

_____

_____

_____

_____

_____

_____

_____

_____

_____

_____

_____

_____

From The Kitchen Of:

_____

Recipe For:

_____

Ingredients:

_____
_____
_____
_____
_____

Directions:

_____
_____
_____
_____
_____
_____
_____
_____
_____
_____

Notes:

_____

_____

_____

_____

_____

_____

_____

_____

_____

_____

_____

_____

_____

_____

_____

_____

From The Kitchen Of:

_____

Recipe For:

_____

Ingredients:

_____

_____

_____

_____

_____

Directions:

_____

_____

_____

_____

_____

_____

_____

_____

_____

_____

_____

Notes:

_____

_____

_____

_____

_____

_____

_____

_____

_____

_____

_____

_____

_____

_____

_____

_____

_____

From The Kitchen Of:

_____

Recipe For:

_____

Ingredients:

_____

_____

_____

_____

_____

Directions:

_____

_____

_____

_____

_____

_____

_____

_____

_____

_____

Notes:

_____

_____

_____

_____

_____

_____

_____

_____

_____

_____

_____

_____

_____

_____

From The Kitchen Of:

_____

Recipe For:

_____

Ingredients:

_____
_____
_____
_____
_____

Directions:

_____
_____
_____
_____
_____
_____
_____
_____
_____
_____

Notes:

_____

_____

_____

_____

_____

_____

_____

_____

_____

_____

_____

_____

_____

_____

_____

_____

From The Kitchen Of:

_____

Recipe For:

_____

Ingredients:

_____

_____

_____

_____

_____

Directions:

_____

_____

_____

_____

_____

_____

_____

_____

_____

_____

_____

Notes:

_____

_____

_____

_____

_____

_____

_____

_____

_____

_____

_____

_____

_____

_____

_____

From The Kitchen Of:

_____

Recipe For:

_____

Ingredients:

_____

_____

_____

_____

_____

Directions:

_____

_____

_____

_____

_____

_____

_____

_____

_____

_____

Notes:

_____

_____

_____

_____

_____

_____

_____

_____

_____

_____

_____

_____

_____

_____

_____

_____

From The Kitchen Of:

_____

Recipe For:

_____

Ingredients:

_____
_____
_____
_____
_____

Directions:

_____
_____
_____
_____
_____
_____
_____
_____
_____
_____

Notes:

_____

_____

_____

_____

_____

_____

_____

_____

_____

_____

_____

_____

_____

_____

From The Kitchen Of:

_____

Recipe For:

_____

Ingredients:

_____

_____

_____

_____

_____

Directions:

_____

_____

_____

_____

_____

_____

_____

_____

_____

_____

Notes:

_____

_____

_____

_____

_____

_____

_____

_____

_____

_____

_____

_____

_____

_____

_____

From The Kitchen Of:

_____

Recipe For:

_____

Ingredients:

_____

_____

_____

_____

_____

Directions:

_____

_____

_____

_____

_____

_____

_____

_____

_____

_____

Notes:

_____

_____

_____

_____

_____

_____

_____

_____

_____

_____

_____

_____

_____

_____

_____

From The Kitchen Of:

_____

Recipe For:

_____

Ingredients:

_____

_____

_____

_____

_____

Directions:

_____

_____

_____

_____

_____

_____

_____

_____

_____

_____

_____

Notes:

_____

_____

_____

_____

_____

_____

_____

_____

_____

_____

_____

_____

_____

_____

_____

_____

From The Kitchen Of:

_____

Recipe For:

_____

Ingredients:

_____

_____

_____

_____

_____

Directions:

_____

_____

_____

_____

_____

_____

_____

_____

_____

_____

Notes:

_____

_____

_____

_____

_____

_____

_____

_____

_____

_____

_____

_____

_____

_____

_____

From The Kitchen Of:

_____

Recipe For:

_____

Ingredients:

_____

_____

_____

_____

_____

Directions:

_____

_____

_____

_____

_____

_____

_____

_____

_____

_____

Notes:

_____

_____

_____

_____

_____

_____

_____

_____

_____

_____

_____

_____

_____

_____

_____

_____

From The Kitchen Of:

_____

Recipe For:

_____

Ingredients:

_____

_____

_____

_____

_____

Directions:

_____

_____

_____

_____

_____

_____

_____

_____

_____

_____

Notes:

_____

_____

_____

_____

_____

_____

_____

_____

_____

_____

_____

_____

_____

_____

_____

_____

From The Kitchen Of:

_____

Recipe For:

_____

Ingredients:

_____

_____

_____

_____

_____

Directions:

_____

_____

_____

_____

_____

_____

_____

_____

_____

Notes:

_____

_____

_____

_____

_____

_____

_____

_____

_____

_____

_____

_____

_____

_____

From The Kitchen Of:

_____

Recipe For:

_____

Ingredients:

_____

_____

_____

_____

_____

Directions:

_____

_____

_____

_____

_____

_____

_____

_____

_____

_____

_____

Notes:

_____

_____

_____

_____

_____

_____

_____

_____

_____

_____

_____

_____

_____

_____

From The Kitchen Of:

_____